· MEET ·
PAUL KLEE

Read With You Center for Excellence in STEAM Education

Read With You

D1262510

ISBN: 979-8-88618-099-2
First Edition January 2022

Persian Nightingales, 1917

In the Spirit of Hoffmann, 1921

Temple Gardens, 1920

Episode before an Arab Town, 1923

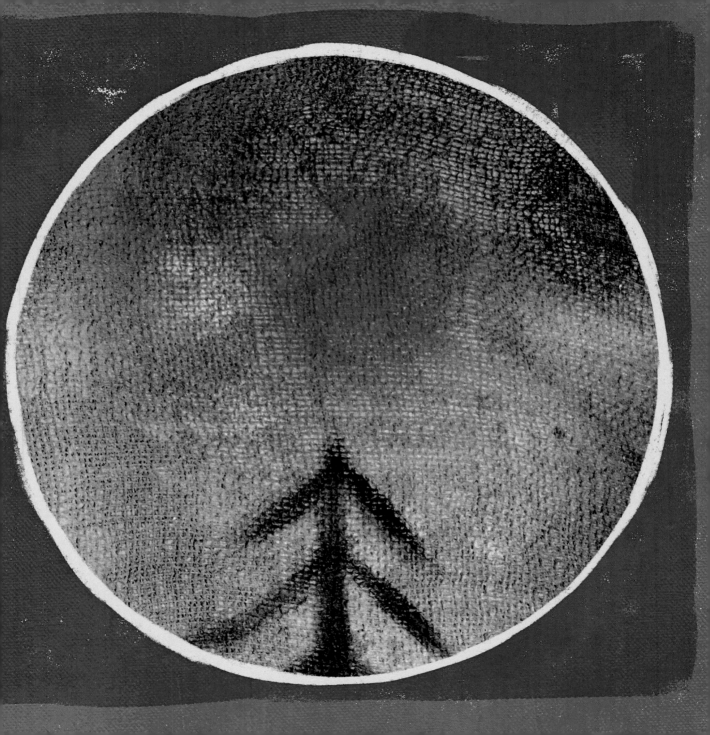

Small Picture of Fir Trees, 1922

Villa R, 1919

Black Columns in a Landscape, 1919

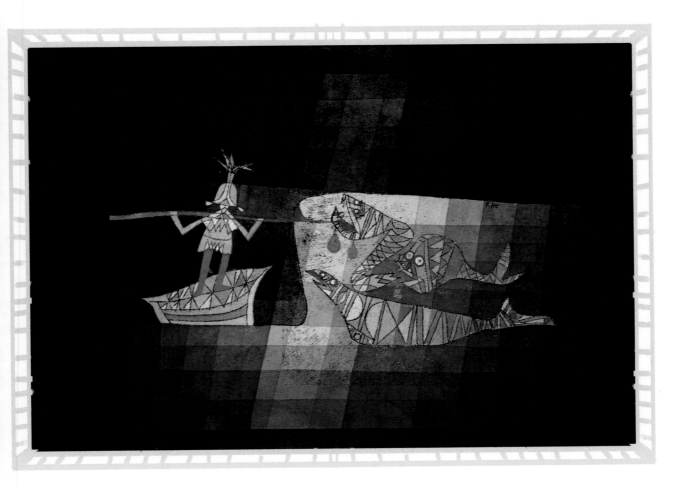

Battle Scene from the Funny and Fantastic Opera, The Seafarers, 1923

Find Examples

This painting is titled *In the Realm of the Air* (1917). Remember, complementary colors are opposite each other on a color wheel.

Ask an adult to show you a color wheel. What complementary colors can you find in this picture?

Triadic colors are any three colors that make a triangle on the color wheel. One example is blue, red, and yellow. Can you find a painting with this set of three colors?

Imagine you want to make a painting with just two colors. What colors would you choose?

Connect

This painting is *Dry Cooler Garden* (1921).

What colors can you find in the painting? What feelings do they make you feel?

What kind of music does this make you think about?

Try playing different songs and see which one matches the painting best.

How many squares can you find in the painting? Look for other paintings in the book that have lots of squares.

Craft

Option 1

1. Choose two complementary colors on the color wheel.

2. Use a pencil to draw a picture full of squares.

3. Color everything in using just those two colors. You can use different shades of your two colors for variety.

Option 2

1. Play your favorite song. Listen to it with your eyes closed and see what colors it brings to mind.

2. Draw a picture with those colors.

Made in United States
North Haven, CT
18 May 2023